Screenwriting

✫ ✫ ✫ ✫ ✫

A PRACTICAL GUIDE TO PURSUING THE ART

✫ ✫ ✫ ✫ ✫

BY JASON SKOG

CONTENT ADVISER
Matthew Mauch, Screenwriting Instructor,
Normandale Community College, Bloomington, Minnesota

READING ADVISER
Alexa L. Sandmann, EdD, Professor of Literacy,
College and Graduate School of Education, Health, and Human Services,
Kent State University

Compass Point Books
151 Good Counsel Drive
P.O. Box 669
Mankato, MN 56002-0669

Printed in the United States of America in Stevens Point, Wisconsin.
032010
005741WZF10

Editor: Jennifer Fretland VanVoorst
Designer: Ashlee Suker
Media Researcher: Svetlana Zhurkin
Library Consultant: Kathleen Baxter
Production Specialist: Jane Klenk

Image Credits
Alamy: Photos 12, 25, 28, Pictorial Press, 20, Wild Places Photography/Chris
Howes, 5; Capstone Press/Karon Dubke, cover; Courtesy of Ralph Tropf, 40;
Courtesy of Robert Festinger, 37; Getty Images: Jason Merritt, 6, The Image Bank/
John Eder, 14; iStockphoto: Aldo Murillo, 16, Arthur Carlo Franco, 12, Bijoy
Verghese, 24, Chris Reed, 42, Chris Schmidt, 13, Igor Balasanov, 9, Juanmonino,
36, Lise Gagne, 35, Rich Legg, 44, Sandy Sandy, 8, Winston Davidian, 39, Zhang Bo,
17, 19; Rex USA/Everett/Warner Bros., 23; Shutterstock: Arena Creative, 30, Biczó
Zsolt, 10, CandyBoxPhoto, 26, David M. Albrecht, 43, Inginsh, 33, Jose AS Reyes, 18,
Ronald Sumners, back cover (background texture) and throughout, Stephen
Coburn, 21, Steve Broer, 4, Stuart Monk, 38, Terry Walsh, 34.

 This book was manufactured with paper containing
at least 10 percent post-consumer waste.

Library of Congress Cataloging-in-Publication Data
Skog, Jason.
   Screenwriting : a practical guide to pursuing the art / by Jason Skog.
      p. cm. — (The performing arts)
   Includes bibliographical references and index.
   ISBN 978-0-7565-4365-5 (library binding)
   1. Motion picture authorship—Vocational guidance—Juvenile
literature. 2. Television authorship—Vocational guidance—Juvenile
literature. I. Title. II. Series.
   PN1996.S475 2011
   808.2'3023—dc22   2010012606

Visit Compass Point Books on the Internet at *www.capstonepub.com*

TABLE OF CONTENTS

You're a Screenwriter

Long before an actor speaks the first word on your favorite TV show or a director shouts "Action!" before shooting a movie scene, somebody wrote something.

Somebody somewhere put pen to paper, pecked away

at a typewriter, or tapped out the story on a computer. Without that person—the screenwriter—there would be no words and no story. And without a story, there would be no TV show and no movie.

For any TV show or movie, it all begins with a script. Like a blueprint for a building or a road map for a trip, a script gives directions for making a movie or television program.

A script shows who is talking, gives the words actors say, and shows how they look, act, dress, and talk. It describes the setting—the time and location—for the movie or show. It also has instructions for actors, directors,

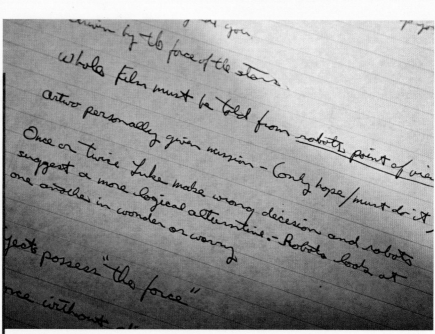

Star Wars, *one of the most beloved films of all time, started as a handwritten script.*

and camera operators, so they can understand the writer's overall idea.

Writing for TV and movies is unlike any other kind of writing. Journalists don't imagine an actor reading one of their articles aloud. Poets, when writing, aren't thinking about readers clapping at the end of their poems. And most book authors don't expect to be thanked at the end of an Academy Awards speech.

While the writing itself is a solitary act, screenwriters have to be flexible and able to work well with others. To make their story a movie or TV

Screenwriter Geoffrey Fletcher won a 2010 Academy Award for Precious, *which he adapted from the book* Push *by Sapphire.*

show requires cooperation among dozens—sometimes even hundreds—of people. Directors, cinematographers, costume designers, set decorators, actors, producers, and studio executives all have ideas based on the script. And those ideas are not always what the writer had in mind.

The screenwriter is in a difficult position because his or her work is publicly presented. And sometimes the public's reaction is less than enthusiastic.

But the writer who sticks it out and succeeds in TV or film is gratified in many ways. The pay can be very high, especially for established writers. There can be awards and praise from peers and the public. And there is the pride in seeing something good you have created become a reality on screen.

Being a screenwriter isn't for everybody. But even if you're just curious about the work, it's worth learning a bit more about this exciting and challenging profession.

Today almost everything you see on TV or in a movie started with a script. The person who wrote it is the screenwriter.

Scripts follow certain rules and are written in special formats. They include specific instructions for actors and directors. And like stories in a book, most scripts have a beginning, a middle, and an end.

Most scripts are written by one person, but occasionally two or three people work together to create a script. Once in a while, there are even more writers.

Screenwriting is a highly specialized skill that can take years to develop. But many of these writers can trace their desire back to when they were young.

Special Skills and Traits

Are you an avid reader? Somebody who has always loved a good story? Perhaps you keep a journal and write for fun. Or are you the kid who just can't wait for your favorite TV show or the premiere of the next big movie?

Whatever interest led you to pick up this book, there are some special skills and traits most screenwriters have had since they were your age. How they became screenwriters

Do you like to dream up stories about interesting people and places? You could have what it takes to be a screenwriter.

varies greatly, but all of them share special qualities that have helped them succeed in their profession.

To become a screenwriter, it helps to have a passion for storytelling. Many screenwriters have enjoyed reading, writing, and watching good stories since they were young. Many also have had a love of the written and spoken word since they were able to read and write. They have a knack for choosing words and putting them together and for writing realistic dialogue.

It also helps to be a good observer. Screenwriters often use their everyday experiences to make their stories more authentic. If you have a curious mind and pay close attention to the world around you—for example, how an ice cream cone tastes after a day at the beach, how the air smells after an early morning rain, or how a bus sounds when it rumbles down the street—then you might make a good screenwriter.

Screenwriters are good at describing the sights, sounds, smells, and flavors of the world around them.

To be a screenwriter, you should also be able to work well with others and deal with criticism and comments on your work. And you have to be strong enough to handle rejection and disappointment if you don't sell a script or get a job right away.

Take Classes

Classes in screenwriting at the middle school and high school levels are rare. Some schools with an arts emphasis may offer introductory classes on the subject.

For the most part, courses in screenwriting don't begin until college. Many schools—especially those with established theater arts programs—offer courses on writing for the screen.

But you can take steps toward becoming a screenwriter without taking college courses. You should take as many writing classes as possible. Practice writing fiction, nonfiction, journalism, and poetry.

Take speech and acting classes to become more familiar with the spoken word. This will help you understand how scripts translate into acting and stage direction. Basic courses on film, television, and theater can help you learn about the entertainment business and how screenwriting fits into the overall framework.

Take any writing classes you can, and practice writing in a variety of genres.

College and Private Instruction

Universities and colleges with film or theater arts programs typically offer courses in screenwriting. Some private conservatories or academies offer screenwriting workshops. Such workshops are usually taught by writers with experience writing for TV or film. Students develop their own ideas for scripts into half-hour sitcoms, hour-long dramas, or even feature-length film scripts, depending on the class.

Some schools offer shorter seminars to give you a basic

idea of screenwriting fundamentals. Try searching the Internet for "screenwriting workshops" to find classes near you or to learn about an online course you might take.

Study at Home or in the Theater

Even if you don't have access to screenwriting classes, you can learn a lot about how movies and TV shows are written just by watching them.

At screenwriting workshops aspiring writers often critique one another's work.

This is not an invitation to veg out with a bowl of popcorn and stare blankly at the screen or fall asleep in a darkened theater. Instead, watch actively and intently. Take notes. Jot down your reactions as the show unfolds. If it's too dark to write in a movie theater, do it as soon as you can afterward. Think about how the story was put together. Write down some of your favorite lines, and think about what made each line stand out for you.

Rent and watch as many kinds of movies as you can.

When you watch a movie, pay attention to the things you like and don't like about the script, and use this information to guide your own writing.

Talk about them with your friends and family. Ask them what they liked, what they didn't like, and why. Think about whether you would have written the script differently or how the story would have been with a different ending.

Read. Read. Read

Published screenplays that have been turned into movies are widely available at libraries and online. Seek out some of your favorite films, and then find their published scripts and read them.

Reading a script shows you the work involved, the formats required, how characters are introduced, how dialogue and stage directions are written, and how scenes change from one to the next. Read as many scripts as you can find.

Better yet, watch the movie and follow along with the script at the same time. You can see how the script influenced the director and actors and think about how you might approach your own screenplay.

To get an idea of how a story is turned into a script, read a novel, play, or short story on which a movie was based. Try to figure out why things in the original story were left out of the movie or handled differently. You might even be able to compare the story with the script and the finished movie.

There are dozens and dozens of books on screenwriting. Visit your library, check some out, and learn what works—and what doesn't—from those who write screenplays for a living.

Write, Write, Write

Like professional golfers practicing putting or basketball players lofting free throws, you only can get better by doing it. Over and over again.

The best way to become a better writer is—no surprise here—by writing.

Check out your local library for books on screenwriting.

Start with short pieces. Start small and build on your ideas. Practice writing bits of dialogue and individual scenes. Take a crack at writing a one-act play or a short film or documentary. Invite your friends or kids from the neighborhood to read your lines or put on a performance.

The more you write, the better at it you will become.

Keep a journal or diary to record things you think and feel, things you see and hear, and things that have happened to you. Your unique experiences and viewpoint provide a world of material that could make for a great script. A journal can come in handy later as you try to develop believable stories, colorful characters, and realistic dialogue.

DO A CHARACTER SKETCH

Character sketches are detailed descriptions of characters in books, movies, plays, or television shows. They describe who the characters are, what they look like, where they're from, how they talk, what they wear, and how they're connected to others.

To write your own character sketch, begin by imagining a character you'd like to have in your story. Start your sketch by describing his or her basic physical features. List the character's height, weight, skin color, eye color, and hair color and style. Include any interesting features, such as tattoos, scars, piercings, and birthmarks.

Describe how he or she walks and talks. Describe the character's general mood and what makes him or her happy, sad, or angry. The more detail you include, the better. Defining what makes your character tick will help you make the character more believable in whatever movie or TV show you put him or her.

Chapter 2

Learning the Job

There are two main kinds of screenplays: original and adapted.

An original screenplay is a work that has been entirely written by the screenwriter. That doesn't mean the work must be entirely fiction. It can be a script based on real events, but it must be the writer's own research and writing. The movie *E.T: The Extra-Terrestrial* had an original screenplay. So did *Titanic*, even though the movie was based on something that really happened.

An adapted screenplay is based on a previously published work, such as a book, play, or magazine article. The screenplay for the movie *Where the Wild Things Are* was adapted from the popular book by Maurice Sendak. And all of the *Harry Potter* movies are adapted screenplays that are based on the popular book series.

The movie Titanic *was based on an actual event, but its screenplay was an original work of art.*

By some estimates, more than half of all movies made since 1920 have been based on plays or novels. If you're not sure you have a good idea for an original screenplay, consider basing yours on something somebody else has written. But if you adapt from previously produced works, you must first contact the publisher for the rights to use that material.

TIME FOR AN AGENT

Agents aren't just for actors these days. Many people who work on the creative side of TV and movies use agents to help keep their careers on track. For screenwriters, agents are especially useful allies. Many studio and network executives won't even bother to read scripts from writers who are not represented by agents.

Agents don't just help screenwriters get their feet in the door. They also can help them negotiate the terms of a deal if a studio or network is interested in their work. Working with an established and recognized agent can be even more useful to a screenwriter, particularly if he or she hasn't yet sold a script.

If you decide to find an agent, steer clear of the agent who will charge a fee to represent you. Legitimate agents are commission-only, meaning they only get paid if you get paid. Usually they are paid about 10 percent of what you earn. If you pay the agent yourself, there's little incentive for him or her to help find you work.

Find an agent by asking friends, relatives, or teachers if they have any connections in the industry. And if so, whether they know any agents who might be willing to take on a new client.

Genres

Most movies and TV shows fit into one of 12 basic categories, which often are called genres. The categories are action, comedy, crime, drama, epic, horror, juvenile, musical, science fiction, thriller, war, and western.

If you're not familiar with all of the genres, try sticking with something you know best. There's an old saying: "Write what you know." That reduces the amount of research you will have to do, and it will make your screenplay more authentic. So before you sit down to write, think about the kinds of movies you enjoy. Which do you best remember? What kind of movie do you see most often?

Movies about kids and for kids are called juvenile films. Examples include *The Sandlot*, *The Sisterhood of the Traveling Pants*, and *Willy Wonka and the Chocolate Factory*.

Perhaps you've got a great sense of humor. Try channeling your funny bone into a script that will leave viewers rolling in the aisles. Or if you have a strong interest in outer space, alien creatures, and *Star Wars* movies, why not let your imagination run wild and take a stab at writing a sci-fi screenplay?

Screenwriters tend to specialize in one or two genres, much like novelists who write mystery after mystery. Few screenwriters can write across all

The Sisterhood of the Traveling Pants *is a popular movie in the juvenile genre.*

genres. At least at the beginning, let your favorite kinds of films and your interests inspire your writing.

Writing on Spec

"Who's Spec and why are we writing about him?" you might ask. Spec is short for "speculation" or "speculative" writing.

Writing on spec means writing something with no guarantee that you will earn anything for your work. That doesn't mean you won't get paid. An original spec script

could sell. But all writers who write on spec hope their work gets them noticed and that it will lead to something better.

Writing on spec is how most young or unknown writers start out. It's a way for them to gain experience and attract attention to their work. If the first spec falls flat, they'll rewrite and revise it. Then they'll write another and another and hope someone bites.

If you are an aspiring TV writer, writing on spec usually means you are writing episodes for shows currently on the air. That means learning the show inside and out.

Many successful screenwriters began their careers by writing on spec.

FINDING YOUR "VOICE"

Some of the most successful and famous screenwriters have a distinct writing style or "voice." You can often recognize a TV show written by Aaron Sorkin by the fast-paced dialogue and clever cultural references. Not many screenwriters have such strong voices, and they aren't necessary. But staying true to your own voice and vision of a screenplay without compromising or trying to impersonate another writer is vital.

If something you've written doesn't sound like something you would ever say or write—or if it too closely resembles somebody else's work—there's a good chance you haven't found your voice. The best way to find it is to keep writing.

Consider the pace and tone of the dialogue as well as the setting and the characters. When your writing begins to flow smoothly and you aren't struggling to get words on your computer screen, you are getting closer to finding your voice.

Dialogue on The West Wing *bears the unique stamp of writer Aaron Sorkin.*

You must know how the characters speak, act, and relate to one another. You must know their background and what motivates them during most episodes.

The more homework you've done, the better your chance of writing an episode that fits with the TV show. But that episode also must be fresh and new and creative enough to attract the attention of those running the show and hiring writers.

Watching TV counts as homework if you are working toward becoming a screenwriter. Paying attention to the details of the show you are watching will help you write an episode on spec.

Performing the Pitch

If you have a script that's attracted the right interest, you might be invited to a pitch meeting with a development executive.

A pitch meeting is when a writer—and perhaps his or her agent—makes his or her best effort to sell a script or the idea for a script.

But it's more than simply telling the executive what the story is about. Strong and successful pitches require enthusiasm and energy and maybe even a bit of acting. Consider taking an acting class to help polish your presentation before you go to a pitch meeting.

If you're interested in becoming a screenwriter, you must start from scratch when writing on spec. You have to come up with an original idea and create the story yourself. You have to develop the characters, the story, the setting, the dialogue, and the changes of scene.

It's not easy to write on spec, but it's really the only place to start if you want to break into the business.

27

Screenwriter Close-Up

Name: Nancy Oliver

Age: 54

Education: BA in English from the University of Massachusetts, Amherst; MA in acting and directing from Florida State University

Credits: Television: the last three seasons of *Six Feet Under* and the first three seasons of *True Blood*
Film: *Lars and the Real Girl*, for which she was nominated for an Academy Award

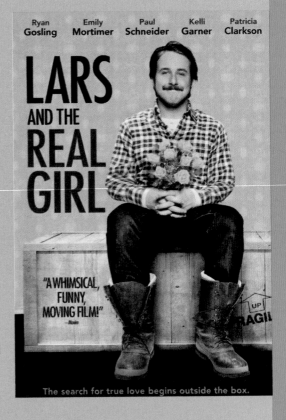

Ryan Gosling Emily Mortimer Paul Schneider Kelli Garner Patricia Clarkson

LARS AND THE REAL GIRL

"A WHIMSICAL, FUNNY, MOVING FILM!"
—*Maxim*

The search for true love begins outside the box.

When did you first become interested in being a screenwriter?
I've always been interested in every kind of writing and have tried them all. Each story you have in your head demands its own form, so when I had an idea that was a movie, I wrote a screenplay. But it took a long time to teach myself to think in cinematic terms. I had to learn to perceive life in a different way, and *Lars* was the first time I even got close to doing it right. I'm more interested in screenwriting now than ever.

What was it like seeing your movie for the first time? It was a mix of excruciating pain and joy. Pain because you're going public, people are seeing your extremely private thoughts and themes on a gigantic screen. Joy because you know how lucky you are and how many deserving people don't get this chance, and how great your actors, director, and producers are. And because, for me, it validated a lifetime of hard work, failure, heartbreak, sacrifice, no money, and obscurity.

What is the best part about being a screenwriter? Even though writing is hard for me and I'm really lazy, I totally enjoy working out the story and making up the characters and figuring out how each one speaks. It's also fun to try to do absolutely the best I can. The other best part is finally having a career, going to parties, wearing great shoes, and getting paychecks.

What advice do you have for young people thinking about becoming a screenwriter?

1. Get your rear end out of the movie theater seat and go participate in your own life with your whole heart and soul and all your senses.

2. Seek out interesting experiences without taking dumb risks.

3. Listen to how people really talk and what they say underneath the words.

4. Think for yourself, and tell the truth.

5. Write.

Many screenwriters started at lower-level jobs on TV shows or movie sets. Many began their career as writer's assistants, running errands or taking notes and making the writer's changes to the script. Assistants are in a good position to learn how a show or movie is put together.

Assistants sit in on story meetings, where writers talk about the overall arc of a coming episode. They sometimes are invited to readings, when actors run through their lines before rehearsal and shooting. And writer's assistants become familiar with the rewriting process that happens after staff writers get notes from studio bosses and network heads.

It can be a long and tedious climb from writer's assistant to staff writer, but it's worth it when the credits roll and your name scrolls across the screen for the first time. You started off making coffee. Now you're making TV shows or movies.

Writing for TV

Writing for a regular television series is considered one of the best writing jobs in Hollywood. It provides a regular, and usually large, paycheck. TV writing is a prestigious and powerful position that can be a lot of fun. It's also one of the hardest to land.

These plum positions tend to go to those who have worked on other shows. Vacancies are often filled by writer's assistants who have toiled by fetching coffee or taking notes in staff meetings.

As good as writing for TV can be, the schedule and expectations can be a grind. There's a new show every week, but without a script, there's nothing. That creates a lot of pressure, so it's not for just any writer.

Writing for half-hour sitcoms and writing one-hour dramas are quite different experiences. Sitcoms tend to

have large writing staffs—as many as 12 to 15 writers—who spend many hours in a conference room telling personal stories and cracking jokes. The stories, jokes, and lines that get the biggest laughs might eventually become part of a script.

For dramas, the writing staff is generally smaller, but writers still meet to discuss an episode's plotline and figure out the overall story arc for the series. When they agree on a direction, the writing is usually done by just one writer or a small team. Other writers might continue to contribute pieces of dialogue or provide feedback.

The Show's Bible

For the TV writer, every show has a bible, a book that includes character names, backgrounds, descriptions, and the overall theme and tone of the show. In some cases it's simply a record of facts and characters based on episodes that have aired. If TV writers don't follow the bible, they risk contradicting something from an earlier episode or having a character do or say something completely out of character. When that happens the audience is left scratching their heads and staff writers have to scramble for solutions.

TV programs and movies are often filmed on a set, an artificial location that serves as a character's living room or some other setting.

Writing for Movies

Being a Hollywood film writer sounds glamorous—working with movie stars, attending fancy premiere parties, accepting prestigious awards.

Unfortunately that's not the reality for most screenwriters. They can go for long stretches without selling a script, relying on other jobs to pay the bills. They must learn to stomach rejection. Repeatedly.

The potential of a big payday and all that comes with it is what helps keep them writing and hustling to sell their

So you've just written the best script that's ever been written. What's next? The life cycle of a script can be long and complicated. Here's what can happen.

Selling—also called shopping—the script usually begins when the screenwriter's agent sends the script to directors and studios. Hollywood is something of a private club, and writers without agents or other connections often have a hard time getting anybody to read their work, let alone produce it.

If a studio likes your script, it might buy it. You'll get paid for your work, but that doesn't mean the script will get made into a movie. It just means the studio will have the option to do so, and nobody else can use the script and make it into a movie.

If the studio green-lights the script, that means it is going to turn the script into a movie. But the work is far from over. The script is likely to go through much revising and rewriting, which you—the original writer—may or may not be a part of.

Even after shooting begins, the script can be changed. Actors sometimes suggest new dialogue, and unforeseen problems can pop up and lead to parts' being added or dropped. Remaining flexible and open to a steady stream of suggestions may be challenging, but it gives you a better chance of being invited to write for more films.

latest script. Even when they make a deal, their **work isn't** over. They can see the script they worked so hard on be revised, rewritten, and sometimes left unrecognizable.

What you see on screen is rarely **exactly what the** original writer wrote. In many cases much of the material has been rewritten. This is because once a script is sold, it becomes the property of the studio. If the studio has different ideas for the production, it can ask for a rewrite.

Rewriting can be done by the original writer, a new writer, or a team of writers. The process can be long and painstaking, but it's something nearly all screenwriters

Most screenplays go through a rewrite process—sometimes by a team of writers working together.

Screenwriters must be able to graciously accept feedback on their work.

must go through. Sometimes the original writer has very little control over how the finished product turns out.

Sometimes large parts of the original material are removed or rewritten. Sometimes characters are replaced or revised. Bits of dialogue are changed, expanded, or condensed. Even the ending can be changed. But if the story remains largely the same, it remains the work of the original writer, who is listed in the credits as the screenwriter.

Because good screenwriters with good scripts are always in demand, new writers are discovered every week in Hollywood. Maybe you'll be one of them.

Screenwriter Close-Up

Name: Robert Festinger

Age: 47

Education: BA in film from New York University

Credits: Films include *In the Bedroom*, for which he was nominated for an Academy Award, and *Trust*

When did you first become interested in writing for film? Probably when I was about 10. I remember my father taking me to all these movies, and thinking about how the actors in the film were talking and responding to each other. And I remember wondering how they got to say those words and who was telling their story.

What was it like seeing one of your films for the first time? It was an amazing thing. In some ways it didn't seem real — these words that were in my head were somehow being spoken by great actors! And then somehow my words become their words.

What is the best part about being a screenwriter? I love to think up new stories, and I love walking around with new characters in my head. It's like walking around having all these interesting, private conversations that no one else knows about.

What advice do you have for young people thinking about becoming a screenwriter? My biggest suggestion is, simply, to write. Write, write, write. I think sometimes we all get ideas and then second-guess them instead of putting them down on the page. But once you do start to work on them, something magical happens. Ideas flow, stories take shape, characters emerge, and worlds open up in ways that can only happen within the writing process. I always say that writing is a collaboration with one's self. Allow for that special collaboration — let your ideas flow and you will be so surprised where they might take you.

Writing for the Stage

As the job title suggests, screenwriters write for the screen, whether it be the large screen of the movie theater or the small screen of the television. But some writers prefer the immediate feedback of live theater. For playwrights, the thrill of seeing their scripts performed and hearing the audience react has no equal.

Writing for the stage is in many ways similar to writing for the screen. But because plays are live, playwrights have unique challenges that TV and movie writers don't have to consider. TV shows and movies, for example, can cut back and forth quickly between scenes and even jump back

New York City's theater district is named for the street that cuts through its center.

Writing a play is usually a more solitary experience than writing for the screen.

and forth in time. This is more difficult to do in a live stage performance. A playwright has to consider whether such quick cuts can be accomplished with a brief lowering of a curtain, for example. As a result plays tend to have fewer settings and time frames. Some plays take place in a single room with just a handful of characters, whose dialogue carries most of the load.

Playwrights also tend to write alone and aren't as subject to as much revising and rewriting. But if they sell a work to a producer, they may see changes made as the production gets under way.

Name: Ralph Tropf

Age: 53

Education: BA in humanities from the University of Central Florida; Equity apprentice at the Burt Reynolds Institute; MFA in theater arts from the University of Nevada, Las Vegas

Credits: Plays include *The Shoe*, *Shadow Hour*, *Public Service*, *21st Century Romance*, and *Squid and Felicity*; executive producer of The All Roses Company

When did you first become interested in being a playwright?
I wrote skits in elementary school and one-act plays in college. I also acted and worked as a technician. At age 29 my first full-length play had several successful readings, and I knew I wanted to write plays exclusively.

What was it like seeing one of your plays performed for the first time? My first full production was in graduate school, and I was horrified. They ruined it! But the production was a success. Over time I learned to appreciate what talented people bring to a play.

What is the best part about being a playwright? I love listening to what people say in the lobby at intermission or after the show, when they don't know I'm listening. When a person doesn't "get" the show, it makes me laugh. When they do, I have the satisfaction of a job well done.

What advice do you have for young people thinking about becoming a playwright? Write a play. Don't say "I want to be a playwright," or "I won't be any good." Just sit down and write one. Join a theater company and help them stage plays. Don't be shy about shoving a script into somebody's hands.

Money, Money, Money

Screenwriters may struggle for years with little pay and recognition. But if a script sells, or they write a big hit, it can mean a lifetime of lucrative work.

There is no minimum price for Hollywood feature film scripts, but Writers Guild guidelines suggest that they be sold for $50,000 to about $100,000. Established screenwriters have sold scripts for $1 million, $2 million, or $3 million and more.

TV writers are typically paid per episode, but the rates vary, depending on the type of show, how long it has been

Protect Your Work

If your work is your own original creation, then it's your property, and it needs to be protected. That way no one else can use it without your permission. For a small fee, you can register your script, and even your idea for a script.

The Writers Guild provides an online registration service. After you sign in, you give your work a title and file name and upload it. A few weeks later, you will receive a certificate verifying that your work has been registered with the guild. If someone uses your registered idea without your permission, you are entitled to compensation.

on the air, and the ratings. Sitcom writers can earn as much as $50,000 for a half-hour episode. Drama writers might earn $100,000 or more for an hour-long script. Full-time staff writers can easily earn well into six figures each year.

For playwrights, pay is more variable. They can sell the royalties to their

A single screenplay can net its writer more than a million dollars, but most scripts sell for much less.

work and be paid a percentage of the box-office receipts. Some established Broadway playwrights earn millions for a play. In other parts of the country, theaters often operate as nonprofit organizations, and lesser known playwrights might earn just $5,000 to $10,000 for a play.

But whatever they are paid, most writers say the process of writing is what keeps them going. They wouldn't do it if they didn't love it.

If you think being a screenwriter or scriptwriter is something you want to pursue, then start taking steps to make it happen.

Do you have to move to Hollywood or New York City to become a successful screenwriter? No, but it helps to be near where most major motion pictures and TV shows are produced. That way you can easily meet with directors and producers, and living in the area shows you're serious about working with them and writing for them.

Wherever you live, take as many writing or writing-related classes as you can find. Watch movies. Go to live

theater. Read books and screenplays that have been produced. Then write and write some more. Revise, edit, and rewrite.

Share your screenplay with your friends and family. Get their reactions. Ask them to perform something you've written. See how your work sounds and looks when performed by others. You'll be surprised when the voices and characters you dreamed up in your head become real before your very eyes.

Invite your friends to perform your screenplay. Hearing how others interpret the words you have written can give you a different perspective on your work.

HANDLING NOTES, FEEDBACK, AND CRITICISM

Even the most respected and established screenwriters in the business crank out a stinker every now and again. That doesn't mean they're bad writers. No star ball player hits a home run every time he or she swings the bat.

If you swing and miss on a screenplay, be prepared to get some notes and criticism from the studio or network. How you respond to those suggestions is a good indication of how you will fare in this profession in the long run.

Consider the notes carefully. If you simply can't agree with the studio or network's directions, it is better to walk away from the project quietly than to raise a big fuss. But accommodating their suggestions will help your standing as a screenwriter. You will gain a reputation as a team player and somebody who is a pleasure to work with.

Let's be honest. Being a screenwriter takes a lot of hard work, dedication, patience, imagination, and a certain amount of luck. The work can be frustrating and demanding, but it can also be exhilarating, rewarding, and inspiring. It's not for everybody, but if you think it's for you, good luck. You'll find a way to write your own ending to the story.

GLOSSARY

arc	continuous line of development
authentic	genuine or real
cinematographers	people who use a movie camera to shoot film
compensation	money paid
dialogue	conversation, especially in a play, movie, TV program, or book
excruciating	severely painful, physically or emotionally
incentive	something that encourages or motivates somebody
legitimate	conforming to accepted rules or standards
lucrative	producing wealth
plotline	main story of a novel, movie, play, or any work of fiction
rights	legal interest in a work of art
royalties	payments to an author for each copy of a work sold
sitcom	humorous television program that features the same group of characters each week; sitcom is short for situation comedy
validated	made worthwhile

READ MORE

Dunkleberger, Amy. *So You Want to Be a Film or TV Screenwriter?* Berkeley Heights, N.J.: Enslow Publishers, 2008.

Hamlett, Christina. *Screenwriting for Teens: The 100 Principles of Screenwriting Every Budding Writer Must Know.* Studio City, Calif.: Michael Wiese Productions, 2006.

Snyder, Blake. *Save the Cat! The Last Book on Screenwriting You'll Ever Need.* Studio City, Calif.: Michael Wiese Productions, 2005.

INTERNET SITES

FactHound offers a safe, fun way to find Internet sites related to this book. All of the sites on FactHound have been researched by our staff.

Here's all you do:

Visit *www.facthound.com*

Type in this code: 9780756543655

INDEX

About the Author

Jason Skog is a freelance writer and author of many books for young readers. He lives with his wife and two young sons in Brooklyn, New York.